Wisdom Tales in an imprint of World Wisdom, Inc.

Library of Congress Control Number: 2022922385

Printed in China on acid-free paper

For information address Wisdom Tales,
P.O. Box 2682, Bloomington, Indiana, 47402-2682
www.wisdomtalespress.com

The Wisdom of Solomon

Demi

❖ Wisdom Tales ❖

In around 990 BCE, King David and Queen Bathsheba had a son. They named him Solomon, which in Hebrew means "peace." One day Solomon would become the king of Israel and rule over a vast kingdom. He would also become fabulously wealthy and wonderfully wise. His father, King David, taught Solomon:

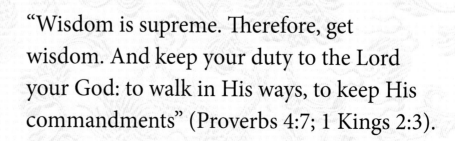

"Wisdom is supreme. Therefore, get wisdom. And keep your duty to the Lord your God: to walk in His ways, to keep His commandments" (Proverbs 4:7; 1 Kings 2:3).

God loved Solomon greatly. One night He appeared to him in a dream and said, "Ask! What shall I give you?"

Solomon answered, "Give to Your servant an understanding heart, that I may discern between good and evil."

God was so pleased with Solomon's answer that He said, "I have given you a wise and understanding heart. And I have also given you both riches and honor, so that there shall not be any one like you among the kings all your days" (1 Kings 3:3-13).

After the death of King David, Solomon became king of Israel. He was soon known throughout the world for his wisdom and his might.

One day the angel Michael brought King Solomon an engraved ring from God. "With this ring you will conquer all the evils of this world, and you will build the most glorious and heavenly temple of the Lord in Jerusalem!"

As soon as King Solomon put on the ring, his powers encompassed everything, including the sun and the moon, the wind and the rain, wisdom and the law, demons and angels, plants and animals.

With the power of God's ring, King Solomon could speak with the animals. He knew the language of the birds of the sky and the fish in the sea.

The animals gathered around King Solomon to learn from his wisdom and compassion. He settled their disputes and they learned to live in peace.

Once, when his soldiers were to engage in battle with King Hiram, King Solomon called upon his friends the eagles to shield his soldiers from the scorching sun. Hundreds of eagles opened their wings, and day seemed to turn into night. King Hiram was so afraid that he retreated and the battle ended before it even began.

King Solomon could even hear the voices of the tiny ants! Once, when an ant soldier was afraid that his army would be stepped upon, King Solomon immediately ordered his own soldiers to go in another direction, thus saving the lives of the entire ant colony.

King Solomon could even hear the voices of the male birds
singing and boasting of their great powers to the female birds.

One day, King Solomon's favorite bird, the hoopoe, said to him: "I have flown to faraway Arabia and have seen the kingdom of Sheba, ruled by a beautiful queen who longs for wisdom and compassion. Allow her to visit your court to learn from your great heart." King Solomon agreed, and the Queen of Sheba journeyed to Jerusalem in a great caravan, carrying precious gifts of gold, silver, rubies, emeralds, diamonds, pearls, spices, monkeys, and even peacocks.

As the Queen of Sheba entered Jerusalem, she saw that it exceeded all the kingdoms of the earth for wealth and riches. She saw thousands of King Solomon's soldiers, all dressed with shields of gold. She saw 40,000 stalls of horses for the king's chariots, and 12,000 horsemen and 12,000 camels of the king's army.

The Queen of Sheba rose to greet the king on his throne. She ascended the six steps, guarded on either side by golden lions, and asked the king all the questions that were in her heart.

Soon she heard that King Solomon exceeded all the kingdoms on the earth for wisdom. For King Solomon spoke many proverbs of wisdom and compassion, and many psalms too with an understanding heart.

King Solomon said:

"To everything there is a season,

A time for every purpose under heaven:

A time to be born, and a time to die;

A time to plant, and a time to pluck what is planted;

A time to kill, and a time to heal;

A time to break down, and a time to build up;

A time to weep, and a time to laugh;

A time to mourn, and a time to dance;

A time to cast away stones, and a time to gather stones;

A time to embrace, and a time to refrain from embracing;

A time to gain, and a time to lose;

A time to keep, and a time to throw away;

A time to tear, and a time to sew;

A time to keep silence, and a time to speak;

A time to love, and a time to hate;

A time of war, and a time of peace" (Ecclesiastes 3:1-8).

The Queen of Sheba carried these great words back to her own people, who greatly rejoiced in their wisdom.

Then King Solomon began to build the great temple of the Lord beside his palace. Giant cedars from Lebanon were cut by 30,000 men, and floated by boats from the kingdom of Tyre to Jerusalem.

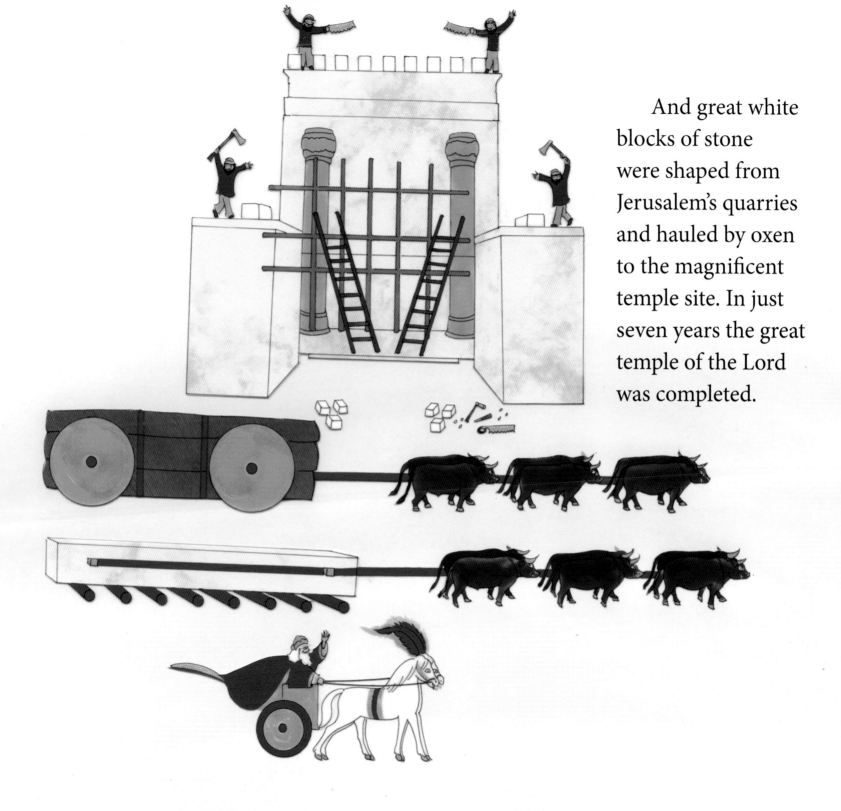

And great white blocks of stone were shaped from Jerusalem's quarries and hauled by oxen to the magnificent temple site. In just seven years the great temple of the Lord was completed.

King Solomon knelt before the altar of the temple and prayed, "Behold, heaven cannot contain You. How much less this temple which I have built! May You hear the supplication of Your servant and of Your people Israel, when they pray toward this place" (1 Kings 8:27-30).

The Lord replied to King Solomon in a dream: "If you walk before Me in integrity of heart and in uprightness, then I will establish the throne of your kingdom over Israel forever" (1 Kings 9:3-6).

After reigning over the Kingdom of Israel for forty years, King Solomon died peacefully in 931 BCE. His wisdom is preserved in the Bible in the books of Proverbs, Ecclesiastes, and the Song of Solomon.

King Solomon's Sayings

"I made my works great, I built myself houses, and planted myself vineyards. I made myself gardens and orchards. I made myself water pools from which to water the growing trees of the grove."

"Then I looked on all the works that my hands had done and on the labor in which I had toiled; and indeed all was vanity and grasping for the wind. There was no profit under the sun" (Ecclesiastes 2:4-11).

"And there is nothing new thing under the sun. I know that whatever God does, it shall be forever. Nothing can be added to it, and nothing taken from it. He has made everything beautiful in its time" (Ecclesiastes 1:9; 3:14; 3:10).

"The sun rises and the sun sets; the wind comes and the wind goes in circuits; all rivers run into the sea and the sea is not full. As no man has power over the wind to contain it, so no man has authority over his day of death" (Ecclesiastes 1:5-7; 8:8).

"But therefore, consider the work of God. He has set eternity in the human heart. Then the dust will return to the earth as it was, and the spirit will return to God who gave it" (Ecclesiastes 7:13; 3:10; 12:7).

"Let us hear the conclusion of the whole matter: fear God and keep his commandments: for this is the whole duty of man" (Ecclesiastes 12:13).

King Solomon on Wisdom

Wisdom is glorious, and never fades away.
-The Wisdom of Solomon 6:12

The fear of the Lord is the beginning of wisdom,
-Proverbs 9:10

Happy is the man who finds wisdom, and the man who gains understanding;
For her proceeds are better than the profits of silver, and her gain than fine gold.
She is more precious than rubies,
And all the things you may desire cannot compare with her.
Length of days is in her right hand, in her left hand riches and honor.
Her ways are ways of pleasantness, and all her paths are peace.
She is a tree of life to those who take hold of her,
And happy are all who retain her.
-Proverbs 3:13-18

The beginning of wisdom is the most sincere desire for instruction,
and concern for instruction is love of her,
and love of her is the keeping of her laws,
and giving heed to her laws is assurance of immortality,
and immortality brings one near to God;
therefore the desire for wisdom brings to the everlasting kingdom.
-The Wisdom of Solomon 6:17-20